MAJOR BATTLES IN US HISTORY

THE BATTLE OF SAN JUAN HILL

FAMOUS BATTLE OF THE SPANISH-AMERICAN WAR

by Bonnie Hinman

FOCUS READERS

WWW.NORTHSTAREDITIONS.COM

Produced for North Star Editions by Red Line Editorial.

Photographs ©: Library of Congress, cover, 1, 29; Red Line Editorial, 5, 23; William Dinwiddie/Library of Congress, 6–7; Schomburg Center for Research in Black Culture/Photographs and Prints Division/From The New York Public Library, 9; Photos.com/Thinkstock, 10; Interphoto/Alamy, 12–13; Hugh L. Scott/Library of Congress/Corbis Historical/VGC/Getty Images, 15; Everett Historical/Shutterstock Images, 17, 18–19, 21; North Wind Picture Archive, 26–27

Content Consultant: Bonnie M. Miller, PhD, Associate Professor of American Studies at University of Massachusetts, Boston

ISBN
978-1-63517-022-1 (hardcover)
978-1-63517-078-8 (paperback)
978-1-63517-182-2 (ebook pdf)
978-1-63517-132-7 (hosted ebook)

Library of Congress Control Number: 2016951033

Printed in the United States of America
Mankato, MN
November, 2016

ABOUT THE AUTHOR

Bonnie Hinman has written more than 40 books, most of them nonfiction. Two of her latest books were *The Mystery of the Nazca Lines* and a biography of President James Monroe. Hinman lives in southwest Missouri with her husband, Bill, and near her children and five grandchildren.

TABLE OF CONTENTS

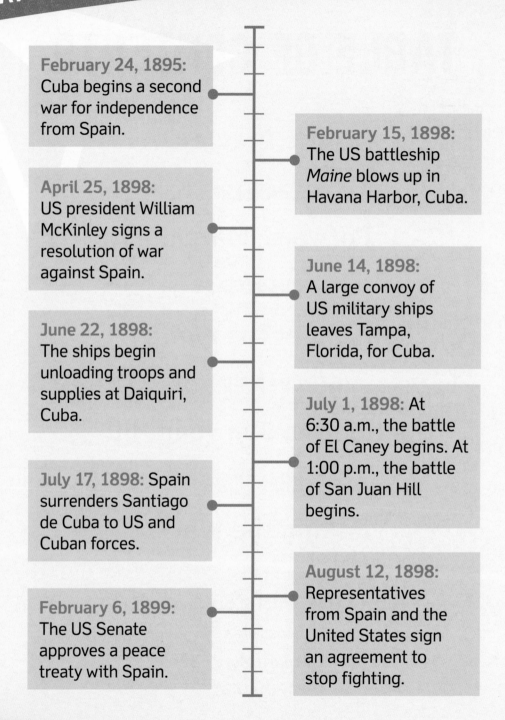

February 24, 1895: Cuba begins a second war for independence from Spain.

February 15, 1898: The US battleship *Maine* blows up in Havana Harbor, Cuba.

April 25, 1898: US president William McKinley signs a resolution of war against Spain.

June 14, 1898: A large convoy of US military ships leaves Tampa, Florida, for Cuba.

June 22, 1898: The ships begin unloading troops and supplies at Daiquiri, Cuba.

July 1, 1898: At 6:30 a.m., the battle of El Caney begins. At 1:00 p.m., the battle of San Juan Hill begins.

July 17, 1898: Spain surrenders Santiago de Cuba to US and Cuban forces.

August 12, 1898: Representatives from Spain and the United States sign an agreement to stop fighting.

February 6, 1899: The US Senate approves a peace treaty with Spain.

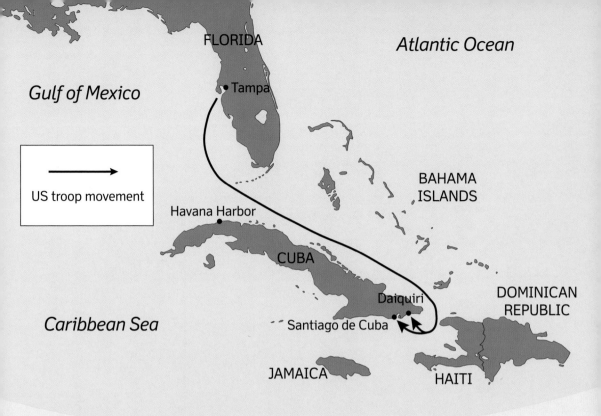

BATTLE OF SAN JUAN HILL

	UNITED STATES	SPAIN
Leader	William Shafter	Arsenio Linares y Pombo
Killed	205	58
Wounded	1,180	170
Captured	0	39

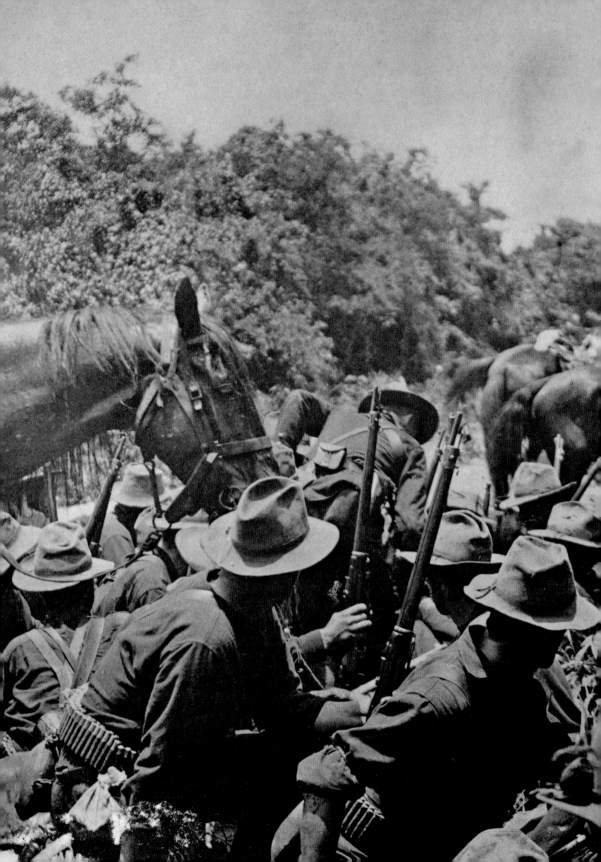

CHAPTER 1

FORWARD, MARCH!

Bullets whistled above as US soldiers lay in the tall grass. They were at the edge of a jungle in Cuba. It was July 1, 1898. The hill-covered landscape was known as the San Juan Heights. Nearly 8,000 US troops were planning to move over the hillside. They hoped to overtake Santiago de Cuba, a Spanish stronghold.

US soldiers duck for cover in a creek bottom near the San Juan Heights.

7

Spanish soldiers stood on top of the hillside. They shot wildly into the crowded grass below. For more than an hour, the US soldiers received no orders to advance or retreat. William Shafter, the general in charge of the US forces, was sick and unable to go to the battlefront. This led to confusion and long delays.

Finally, Shafter's orders reached the regiments. The orders instructed the regiments to charge up Kettle Hill and San Juan Hill of the San Juan Heights. Soldiers bunched together to begin moving up Kettle Hill. Members of the **cavalry** left behind their horses. They needed to fight dismounted. The soldiers

US soldiers charge toward a Spanish fortification on San Juan Hill.

struggled through the waist-high grass. Spanish bullets cut some US soldiers down. But other soldiers climbed higher and higher up the hill. As the soldiers advanced, three US Gatling guns opened fire on the Spanish troops.

THE GATLING GUN

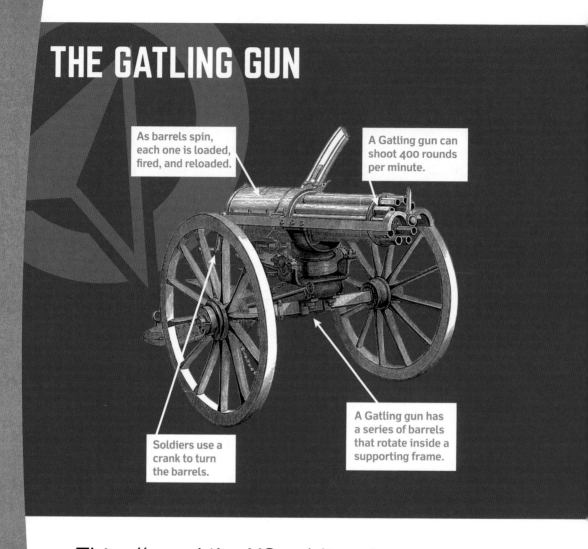

As barrels spin, each one is loaded, fired, and reloaded.

A Gatling gun can shoot 400 rounds per minute.

Soldiers use a crank to turn the barrels.

A Gatling gun has a series of barrels that rotate inside a supporting frame.

This allowed the US soldiers to move more freely up the hill.

Rifle fire lit up the top of the hills as the Spanish stood their ground.

But eventually the Spanish fled their positions. They ran west toward Santiago de Cuba. The US troops reached the crest of the San Juan Heights. But it was not a safe place for them to stay. Shafter feared the Spanish might **counterattack** with **reinforcements**. Shafter gave the order to dig in. The exhausted soldiers began to build **trenches** to help protect themselves against a Spanish attack.

The Spanish sent a small assault. But it was easily defeated. The battle of San Juan Hill was over. The cost was great, with 205 Americans killed and 1,180 wounded. The Spanish toll was 58 men killed and 170 wounded.

CHAPTER 2

REMEMBER THE MAINE!

Spain had ruled Cuba since Christopher Columbus arrived on the island in 1492. But many Cubans wanted to run their own government. They first started fighting for independence in 1868. But by 1878, Spain had put down the revolution. After the war, Spain promised to give Cubans freedom to run their own country.

Cuban fighters gather together to declare their independence from Spain.

However, most of the promised changes never happened. On February 24, 1895, a new revolution began.

The revolution in Cuba was not a war of big battles. Cuban fighters ambushed Spanish troops rather than confronting them in battle. The revolution dragged on. In early 1896, Spain sent General Valeriano Weyler y Nicolau to take charge of the Spanish forces. Weyler ordered **rural** Cuban citizens to move to camps near military headquarters. He believed moving the citizens would keep them from feeding and housing the rebels.

Weyler did not provide enough food or shelter for the people in the camps.

Many displaced Cubans were forced to live in concentration camps with few comforts.

Soon, people became hungry and sick. Approximately 400,000 people were forced into the camps, and nearly 95,000 died there. US journalists reported on the conditions in the camps.

In response, many Americans demanded the United States go to war to free Cuba from Spanish rule. However, some US leaders were concerned a war with Spain might lead to war with other countries. Spanish leaders knew that fighting a war across the Atlantic Ocean would be difficult. But the leaders of Spain did not want to lose their **colony**.

On February 15, 1898, the US battleship *Maine* was in Havana Harbor, Cuba. At 9:40 p.m., two explosions ripped through the ship, killing more than 260 Americans. There was no proof Spain had anything to do with the sinking. But some US newspapers ran headlines saying

The *Maine* exploded in Havana Harbor in February 1898. The cause of the explosion was unclear.

Spain had blown up the ship. "Remember the *Maine*" became a rallying cry. Then, on April 25, 1898, US president William McKinley signed a war resolution. The Spanish-American War (1898) had begun.

CHAPTER 3

THE ROAD TO SAN JUAN HILL

McKinley called for 125,000 volunteers to join the US Army. Men across the United States enlisted. Theodore Roosevelt quit his job as assistant secretary of the navy in order to recruit men for a cavalry regiment. The regiment became known as the Rough Riders.

Theodore Roosevelt (standing, center) with his regiment of Rough Riders

McKinley put Major General William Shafter in charge of the invasion army. Shafter sent all regiments to Tampa, Florida. A large convoy of ships left Tampa on June 14, 1898, carrying 819 officers and 16,058 enlisted men.

The ships headed to Santiago de Cuba on the southeast coast of Cuba. Spanish admiral Pascual Cervera y Topete had led his ships into the harbor at Santiago de Cuba to get fuel and other supplies. The US ships formed a **blockade** to keep Cervera's ships in the harbor. If US soldiers and Cuban rebels could capture Santiago de Cuba on land, the Spanish would be unable to escape.

US troops in Tampa, Florida, embark for Cuba.

On June 22, US ships began unloading troops at Daiquiri, a small coastal village east of Santiago de Cuba. It took several days to get the soldiers ashore. Several army units went ahead of the rest and marched to Siboney, Cuba. This village was on the road to Santiago de Cuba.

Mule trains tried to bring food and other supplies to the forward locations. But flooded streams and sticky mud slowed their progress. Most of the soldiers who camped at Siboney had only salted meat and biscuits to eat.

Shafter planned to first capture El Caney, Cuba. This small village was 6 miles (9.7 km) north of Santiago de Cuba. Then Shafter planned to take the San Juan Heights. Approximately 500 Spanish soldiers defended El Caney. Shafter believed the tiny town could be captured in two hours. Then the US troops would join the main force to attack the San Juan Heights.

SPANISH-AMERICAN WAR BATTLES

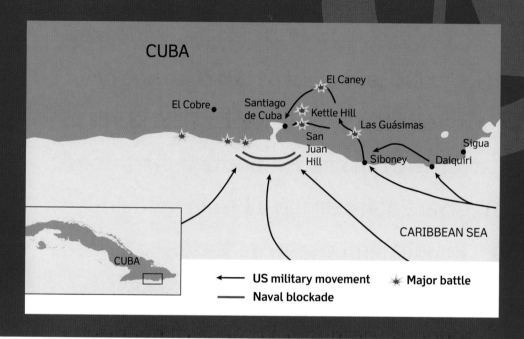

CUBA

El Caney

El Cobre

Santiago de Cuba

Kettle Hill

Las Guásimas

Sigua

San Juan Hill

Siboney

Daiquiri

CARIBBEAN SEA

CUBA

⟵ US military movement   ✴ Major battle
— Naval blockade

Shafter's battle plan soon fell apart.
On July 1, Spanish defenders held El
Caney for 10 hours before retreating.
Meanwhile, the main force of US soldiers
had advanced west along jungle trails.

This group stopped to the east of the San Juan Heights. The soldiers had been ordered to wait for the troops from El Caney before attacking the San Juan Heights. It was a costly order. As the US soldiers waited in tall grass, Spanish soldiers peppered them with bullets from the San Juan Heights.

At 1:30 p.m. on July 1, the US regiments finally received orders to advance. Members of all-black regiments ran beside soldiers from white regiments. The US soldiers soon captured the hills. But it was not a total victory. Shafter had intended to capture Santiago de Cuba, too. Instead, the US forces stayed on the hills and did not continue their advance. The Spanish army was much stronger in Santiago de Cuba. The US would have to lay **siege** to the city.

BUFFALO SOLDIERS

During the Spanish-American War, black soldiers were often called "buffalo soldiers." Despite discrimination, they served bravely on the battlefield.

3,000
black soldiers traveled to Cuba.

1,250
black soldiers fought in the battle of San Juan Hill.

26
black soldiers lost their lives in the battle.

5
black soldiers were awarded the Medal of Honor for bravery.

CHAPTER 4

ENDING THE WAR

On July 3, Cervera and the Spanish fleet tried to exit Santiago de Cuba's harbor. The US blockade stopped and destroyed the Spanish fleet. Two weeks later, Spain surrendered Santiago de Cuba. Then, on August 12, 1898, Spain signed an **armistice**, ending fighting in the Spanish-American War.

Sailors abandon a Spanish naval ship during the battle of Santiago de Cuba.

The United States signed a peace **treaty** with Spain later in 1898. Spain gave up control of its overseas colonies, including Cuba, Puerto Rico, and Guam. It also sold the Philippines to the United States. The deal was a major victory for the United States, which for the first time had overseas colonies. Many Americans welcomed these additions, but some criticized the United States' new role. And Filipinos who had hoped for independence once Spain was defeated took up arms against their new colonizer, the United States.

Many Cubans celebrated the win over Spain. But tensions grew when the

Filipino soldiers march in formation during the rebellion against US rule.

United States occupied Cuba starting in 1899. In 1903, the US and Cuban governments signed an agreement that ended the occupation. But the agreement allowed the United States to have a big role in Cuban affairs, causing lasting tension between the two countries.

FOCUS ON
THE BATTLE OF SAN JUAN HILL

Write your answers on a separate piece of paper.

1. What events led to the Spanish-American War?

2. What mistakes do you think the US troops made during the battle of San Juan Hill?

3. Which city did Shafter hope to capture first?
- **A.** Santiago de Cuba
- **B.** San Juan
- **C.** El Caney

4. Which of these do you think was a common criticism of the United States following the Spanish-American War?
- **A.** The United States was not harsh enough in its treaty with Spain.
- **B.** The United States withdrew from Cuba too quickly, hurting the Cuban people.
- **C.** The United States fought against Spain but took on a role like Spain's in the Philippines.

Answer key on page 32.

GLOSSARY

armistice
An agreement to temporarily stop fighting.

blockade
The closing off of a place to prevent entrance or exit.

cavalry
A military force with troops who serve on horseback.

colony
An area controlled by a country that is far away.

counterattack
An attack made in response to an enemy's attack.

reinforcements
An additional supply of soldiers.

rural
Having to do with the countryside.

siege
An attack in which soldiers surround a town or building.

treaty
An official agreement between groups.

trenches
Narrow ditches in the ground that serve as shelters.

TO LEARN MORE

BOOKS

Amoroso, Cynthia. *William McKinley.* North Mankato, MN:
The Child's World, 2008.

Baker, Brynn. *Roosevelt's Rough Riders.* North Mankato,
MN: Capstone, 2015.

Jurmain, Suzanne. *The Secret of the Yellow Death.*
New York: Houghton Mifflin Harcourt, 2014.

NOTE TO EDUCATORS

Visit **www.focusreaders.com** to find lesson plans,
activities, links, and other resources related to this title.

INDEX

Answer Key: 1. Answers will vary; **2.** Answers will vary; **3.** C; **4.** C

3 1170 01031 6887